Good Night Stories for Rebel Girls

Tales of Extraordinary Women

Once upon a time, a woman named **AMELIA EARHART** climbed into her bright red plane and flew across the ocean, all by herself. It was a brave thing to do, and Amelia was the first woman to do it!

All over the world and all throughout time, women have dared, dreamed, and discovered. Some ruled as queens. Some explored the oceans. And some spoke out for equality. Here are just a few.

Long ago, **CLEOPATRA** was in charge.
Powerful and wise, she ruled ancient Egypt.

GRACE O'MALLEY sailed the seas. Clever and proud, she was the captain of her own ship.

MAE JEMISON's ship was a spaceship! With a *whoosh*, she rocketed straight into the sky. Surrounded by stars, she saw Earth from far, far away.

YAA ASANTEWAA fought for her people. Strong and daring, she was the warrior queen of the Asante Kingdom.

JANE AUSTEN used words to bring stories to life—even when people said women shouldn't be writers.

MILLO CASTRO ZALDARRIAGA used drums to bring music to the world—even when people said girls couldn't be drummers.

When **JOAN JETT** strummed her guitar, she played loud and fast. "I love rock and roll," she shouted to the crowds. And they shouted back!

MALALA YOUSAFZAI loved to read, write, and learn. She raised her voice to make sure every girl around the world could go to school.

RUTH BADER GINSBURG raised her voice to ask tough questions. Why? How? Who? When? She made sure women were treated equally to men.

HARRIET TUBMAN was a courageous leader. She guided hundreds of enslaved people to freedom.

MARIE CURIE was a brilliant scientist.
Her discoveries saved
millions of lives.

JANE GOODALL lived in the jungle. She learned to talk to chimpanzees and shared their stories with the world.

MARIA SIBYLLA MERIAN studied insects. She showed people that wriggly caterpillars turned into beautiful butterflies!

FRIDA KAHLO made colors come alive. With each *swish* of her paintbrush, she created worlds full of animals, flowers, and feelings.

MARGARET HAMILTON used her computer skills to send astronauts safely to the moon.

YUSRA MARDINI used her swimming skills to push a boat full of people safely to the shore.

When **ROSA PARKS** was told that Black people couldn't sit on the bus, she sat right down and demanded change.

When **MANAL AL-SHARIF** was told that women couldn't drive, she got in the car and—*vroom!* She went for a ride.

SIMONE BILES broke records as she flipped through the air. She also rewrote the rules—reminding everyone about the power of practicing hard, having fun, and being kind to yourself too.

Countless Rebel women have faced their fears, opened their hearts, and forged their own paths.

The Cholita Climbers scaled huge mountains—in their colorful skirts.

Xian Zhang waved her hands and turned sounds into symphonies.

Wang Zhenyi taught herself—and the world—about the sun, moon, and stars!

Helen Keller learned to sign and speak—and speak up for others.

Misty Copeland spun, stretched, and soared across the stage.

So what do you **THINK**?
What will you **DO**?

When you close your eyes at night, dream of all the **ADVENTURES** you will go on and all the exciting things you will **LEARN**.

And remember, whether you sail or sing, plant seeds or pass laws, always be uniquely you.

YOU ARE A REBEL GIRL TOO

Black Rabbit Books | P.O. Box 227 | Mankato, MN 56001
www.blackrabbitbooks.com

Library edition published in 2026 by Black Rabbit Books.
This library-bound edition is reprinted by arrangement with Rebel Girls, Inc.

Cataloging-in-Publication Data is available at the Library of Congress.
ISBN 978-1-64582-572-2

Printed in China

Text by Sarah Parvis and Abby Sher | Art Direction by Giulia Flamini | Design by Kristen Brittain
Based on *Good Night Stories for Rebel Girls* by Elena Favilli and Francesca Cavallo

Illustrations: Giulia Flamini (Earhart), Kiki Ljung (Cleopatra), Kathrin Honesta (O'Malley), Alexandra Bowman (Jemison), Noa Snir (Asantewaa), Sophia Martineck (Austen), Sarah Wilkins (Zaldarriaga and Cholita Climbers), Annalisa Ventura (Jett), Sara Bondi (Yousafzai), Eleanor Davis (Ginsburg), Sally Nixon (Tubman and Parks), Claudia Carieri (Curie), Emmanuelle Walker (Goodall), Amanda Hall (Merian), Helena Morais Soares (Kahlo), Édith Carron (Hamilton), Jessica Cooper (Mardini), Kate Prior (al-Sharif), Eline Van Dam (Biles), Ping Zhu (Zhang and Copeland), Monica Garwood (Keller), Ana Galvañ (Wang)